IMAGES
of America
AROUND AND ABOUT
BASKING RIDGE
LIBERTY CORNER
AND LYONS

Bernards Township, from the *Atlas of Somerset County, N.J.* (Beers, Comstock & Cline, NY, 1873). The area included Basking Ridge, Liberty Corner, Lyons, Bernardsville, and Far Hills, with a total population of 2,369. Somerset County's population was 21,994. Far Hills became an independent municipality in 1921, and Bernardsville in 1924. (Bernards Township Library)

IMAGES
of America

AROUND AND ABOUT
BASKING RIDGE
LIBERTY CORNER
AND LYONS

June O. Kennedy

ARCADIA

First published 1995
Copyright © June O. Kennedy, 1995

ISBN 0-7524-0099-1

Published by Arcadia Publishing,
an imprint of the Chalford Publishing Corporation
One Washington Center, Dover, New Hampshire 03820
Printed in Great Britain

Library of Congress Cataloging-in-Publication Data applied for

The Basking Ridge Fire Company No. 1 auto pauses before the Old Oak Tree at the Presbyterian Church, 1910. (George L. Frost Collection)

Contents

Acknowledgments

As research began on this work, there was a groundswell of cooperation from people offering photographs. The feeling was one of jubilation that a book with pictures of their neighborhoods would surface. Folks called classmates and friends; this networking has resulted in *Around and About Basking Ridge, Liberty Corner, and Lyons*. Searches in attics, albums, and closets uncovered the most interesting and cherished pictures of the past. Residents may have relocated, but they stayed in touch. Memories have not dimmed.

More than sixty persons generously gave their thoughts, time, and treasures to me. They include: Rosemary Allen, William Allen, Mario Allenzo, Janet C. Arleo, the William Beatty III family, Jonathon Booth, Priscilla C. Bruno, Howard A. Brush, Constance Carlson, Ransford G. Crane, James DeCoste, the DeCoster sisters, Phyllis B. Domanski, Shirley Ehrenberg, Woodruff English, Carmen A. Fortenbacker, James Henry, the E.V. Hicks family, Jean and Homer Hill, Herbert Hilmer Jr., Alan Jaquish, Deborah Juterbock, Fred Kampmier III, William J. Kearns, Mary G. Kenney, Nancy C. Knobloch, Philip Koechlein, George Lee III, Orrin Lincoln, Carolyn G. Malfatone, Lois G. Martin, June S. Martratt, J. Donald McArthur, Janet H. McGahey, Peter S. Palmer, Mae S. Ruggerio, Mary C. Ruggerio, Qaaim Saalik, William L. Scheuerman III, Paul Sempf, Agnes D. Sheehan, Elizabeth R. Sigler, Elizabeth K. Sisto, Douglas Sloss, Helen T. Smith, Laurence Smith, Marion G. Stadtmueller, Louis L. Sutro, Denise Szabo, Marion D. Turner, Mildred D. Van Dyke, and Elizabeth G. Wolsky. The collections of George L. Frost and Charles Wickenhaver also were used.

My appreciation to the *Abbeville Press*, Basking Ridge Garden Club, Bernards Township Library, Bernardsville Library Local History Room, *Bernardsville News*, Bonnie Brae, Independence National Historical Park, League of Women Voters Somerset Hills, Lord Stirling School, Massachusetts Historical Society, The Historical Society of Somerset Hills, and the Township of Bernards.

What an unforgetable experience it has been to meet these townpeople who cherish their roots and ancestors. The knowledge, materials, and remembrances gathered are the fabric of this book. It has been my pleasure to use these resources to present this pictorial history of Basking Ridge, Liberty Corner, and Lyons.

June O. Kennedy

References

Historical Booklet Committee. *Historical Booklet of Bernards Township, N.J.* Published to commemorate the Bicentennial, 1760–1960. Basking Ridge: Historical Booklet Committee, May 1960.

Bernards Township. *Inventory of Historically Significant Buildings in Bernards Township.* Bernards Township Report #1.470. Bernards Township: April 18, 1979.

Introduction

"Our history is the source of our strength and is what makes America great."

Abraham Lincoln

Basking Ridge, Liberty Corner, and Lyons are places in Bernards Township, a municipality 9 miles long, 3 miles wide, with an area of 23.2 square miles. Immigrants from Scotland and northern Ireland settled the area; John Harrison, agent of King James III, purchased 3,000 acres from the Lenni Lenape Indians in 1717, and William Penn eventually bought 7,000 more acres. These two acquisitions formed the nucleus of the Township. As the number of settlers increased, the presence of Indians in the area began to diminish, until it disappeared almost entirely (a major Indian dwelling place was once located at the present North Maple Avenue, Madisonville Road site of AT&T).

The names of the early residents are reflected in streets, roads, schools, and buildings. It is difficult to imagine Basking Ridge, Liberty Corner, and Lyons as part of a larger territory—the Bernards map included Warren until 1806, Far Hills until 1921, and Bernardsville until 1924. Records as early as the mid-eighteenth century cite addresses in Basking Ridge, Liberty Corner, and Lyons.

Bernards Township was chartered in 1760 by King George II and named in honor of Sir Francis Bernard, who was royal governor from 1758–1760, possibly for his diplomacy in settling the French and Indian Wars.

Basking Ridge's main road, Finley Avenue, is dotted with centuries-old trees and buildings from various architectural periods now used as shops, restaurants, and businesses. The Presbyterian Church is the focal point of the village. The entire area figured greatly in the American Revolution: General Lee's arrest occurred at the Widow White's Tavern; General Washington visited Lord Stirling's estate; William Annin quartered troops of Lafayette in his stone house; the triumphant French marched through Liberty Corner; the Basking Ridge military hospital cared for many wounded soldiers; and under the ancient oak tree of the Presbyterian Church are buried thirty-five veterans.

In 1795 the Reverend Robert Finley continued the work of his predecessor, Reverend Dr. Samuel Kennedy, and conducted the Basking Ridge Classical School, which prepared young men for the College of New Jersey (Princeton). In 1809 a brick academy was built, later claimed by historians as "contributing more men to the bar, the bench, and the pulpit." Two students gained national prominence as vice-presidential candidates: Theodore Frelinghuysen (with Henry Clay in 1844) and William L. Dayton (with John C. Fremont in 1856). U.S. Representative Henry Southard and his son, U.S. Senator Samuel L. Southard, an academy graduate, were the first father-son team to serve in the U.S. Congress. The younger Southard later became the governor of New Jersey. Other interesting figures in the area's history include Mary Lewis Kinnan, a local heroine rescued from Indian captivity; Dr. Horatio Gates Whitnall, a Civil War surgeon; Colonel John Jacob Astor and his son, John Jacob Astor VI; Samuel and William Childs, brothers of Childs Restaurant fame; and Samuel Owen, the pharmaceutical magnate.

Liberty Corner, a rural area, had the services of Dominie James T. English, first pastor of its Presbyterian Church, for thirty-eight years after his arrival in 1838 (his descendants still reside in the family homestead). Following the Civil War, the village became a popular vacation resort; visitors were housed at farms and lodgings. Fresh dairy products and produce were shipped to hotels in Newark and New York daily. The Fellowship Deaconry, a non-denominational center, was established in 1933, and Liberty Corner is also the headquarters of the U.S. Golf Association. The relaxed pace of Liberty Corner is evident in its main thoroughfare, Church Street, a microcosm of nineteenth-century structures in a rezoned business region.

Lyons, the territory which includes the U.S. Veterans Hospital, runs from the railroad station environs at Lyons Road (formerly Clairvaux Road) and Stone House Road. The century-old stone quarry was a major employer in the 1920s, and continues in full operation. Several large dairy farms also operated here. The former Coppergate Farm, an equestrian riding stable, was at one time Day Farm. The Veterans Hospital, created by an act of the 68th Congress, opened its doors as a major psychiatric hospital in 1930, and its last Spanish-American War veteran died in 1939. Lyons is remembered for its working families and farms.

Education played a dominant role in the villages. Because at one time there was no public instruction in New Jersey, small private academies taught students who could afford their fees. In 1853 district schools were established.

Slavery figured in Bernard's past. There are slave burial areas in both the Basking Ridge and Liberty Corner Presbyterian cemeteries. Nathan Woodward, the last slave in Basking Ridge, died in 1901 at age 110. Following a detailed investigation, the two brick buildings on the site of Lord Stirling's Basking Ridge estate were reclassified from slave quarters to auxiliary outbuildings, erected from the debris of the manor house.

The arrival of the railroad in 1872 with depots at Basking Ridge and Lyons led to residential development, since the citizens of Basking Ridge, Liberty Corner, and Lyons now were able to work away from home. Many churches were established, providing inspiration and comfort to worshippers. Mills and stores flourished, and Basking Ridge became a thriving village surrounded by farms. The railroad brought in visitors anxious to experience the clean country air and natural beauty of the area, and soon a thriving "tourist trade" existed.

Around and About Basking Ridge, Liberty Corner, and Lyons contains photographs of patriots, service personnel, school children, police and firemen, and fraternal and religious groups portraying pride in their community. From colonial times to the post-World War II era, these are the proud people who have called Basking Ridge, Liberty Corner, and Lyons home. There are photographs of places that no longer exist; citizens working during hard economic times; progress and development; commerce and industry; weddings and parties; babies and grandparents. There are railroad stations, early autos and planes, general stores, and vintage fashions.

Most of all, *Around and About Basking Ridge, Liberty Corner, and Lyons* is a tribute to the families who lived there and made these places special. This leads one to interpret there is "no place like home." If it were not for love of the land and faith in the future, there would not be the wealth of knowledge available from people who called Basking Ridge, Liberty Corner, and Lyons home.

June O. Kennedy
May 25, 1995

One
Basking Ridge

Main Street, Basking Ridge, N. J.

Main Street, 1908. The main thoroughfare was renamed Finley Avenue in 1912 to honor the Reverend Robert Finley, fifth pastor of the Basking Ridge Presbyterian Church and director of the Basking Ridge Classical School. (Mildred Dunham Van Dyke)

The Basking Ridge Railroad Station, c. 1890. Stationmaster Joe Buck is one of the men in front. The building burned April 4, 1911. (The Historical Society of the Somerset Hills)

The Basking Ridge Railroad Station, c. 1915, replaced the original depot shortly after the fire. The stucco structure, somewhat Spanish Colonial in design, has tile roofing and exposed bracket trusses under the eaves. (Mildred Dunham Van Dyke)

The Basking Ridge Presbyterian Church, 1911. The church of Greek Revival architecture was built in 1839 and rests on the site of two former edifices, a log cabin and wooden building, dating back to about 1717. In 1892 the original boxed pews were removed. This house of worship is the dominant feature of the village and was the building around which the village developed and still revolves. It is listed on the State and National Registers of Historic Places. (The Historical Society of the Somerset Hills)

Reverend and Mrs. Lauren Bennett in front of the Presbyterian Church manse, c. 1920. Reverend Bennett was pastor from 1913 to 1944. (Mildred Dunham Van Dyke)

PRESBYTERIAN CHURCH,
BASKING RIDGE, N. J.,
Thursday Afternoon, Nov, 7th '89.

LECTURE
TO LADIES ONLY.

---BY---

Dr. Mary F. Newgeon
OF NEW YORK.

SUBJECT :
The Perils and Possibilities
of American Womanhood

MANY WRONGS WHICH SHOULD BE RIGHTED; NON-COMPATIBILITY IN MATRIMONY; DANGERS AND CONSEQUENCES WHICH RESULT THEREFROM; THE PHILOSOPHY OF BODILY SYMMETRY, HEALTH AND VIGOR; HOW TO CURE DISEASE PROLONG LIFE AND AVOID THE INFIRMITIES OF OLD AGE.

This Lecture will be illustrated with life-size paintings, will be highly instructive and entertaining to both old and young. Attendance of intelligent and sound thinking ladies especially invited.

Lecture to Ladies Only, 1889. Flyers were distributed throughout the village, announcing this lecture concerning feminine topics for women only. Admission was free. (The Historical Society of the Somerset Hills)

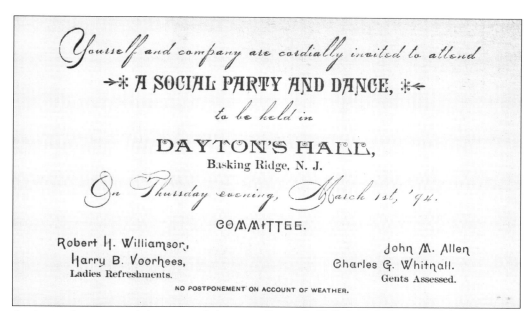

An invitation to a social party and dance at Dayton's Hall, March 1, 1894. (The Historical Society of the Somerset Hills)

Dayton's Hall, 1900. The hall stood just below the Presbyterian Church cemetery on North Finley Avenue and was used for graduations, socials, dances, plays, and other events. A second floor was added after 1910. The hall was later used as a garage and car agency. In 1942 it was purchased to allow additional church parking and demolished. (The Historical Society of the Somerset Hills)

Julia Allen Holmes and John Holmes (second row, first two people from the left) with relatives at the Holmes family homestead on Lake Road, *c*. 1890. (William Allen)

The Basking Ridge village green, *c*. 1899, during the gas light era. (Marion D. Turner)

Dr. Horatio Gates Whitnall, *c.* 1900, owned land from the west line of properties on Brownlee Place and South Finley Avenue across the railway line and down to Harrison's Brook. The Whitnall farm was site of the present Oak Street School. Dr. Whitnall, a Civil War Union Army surgeon, lived at 123 South Finley Avenue and donated his automobile to the local fire company. (The Historical Society of the Somerset Hills)

Charles Wickenhaver, *c.* 1904, a Basking Ridge contractor at his East Lewis Street farm. A fire at another barn in 1903 resulted in the total loss of its contents, including four horses, and prompted the organization of the Basking Ridge Fire Company in 1904. (Charles Wickenhaver Collection)

Mrs. Calvin Thompson, *c.* 1870. Mrs. Thompson, nee Margaret Voorhees, married a prosperous farmer with dairy cattle in the Madisonville area. (Mildred Dunham Van Dyke)

Stylish women enjoying an outdoor chat on Main Street (South Finley Avenue), 1910. From left to right are Bess Stone, Dorothy Wing, Jane Dunham, and Katherine Ellis. St. Mark's Chapel is on the left, with the Voorhees house to the rear. (Mildred Dunham Van Dyke)

Charles and Mary Wickenhaver with their daughter Mabel, *c.* 1898, in front of their home at 140 South Finley Avenue. There was a stone wall along the front. The property was acquired by St. Mark's Church for a manse, and later moved back for a new church. (Charles Wickenhaver Collection)

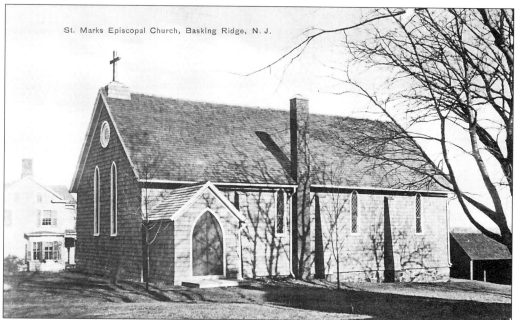

St. Marks Episcopal Church, Basking Ridge, N. J.

St. Mark's Chapel, 1909. The oldest Episcopal house of worship in the Somerset Hills was built in 1852 and assumed independent status in 1950. A larger church was constructed next to it at the corner in 1969, with the manse relocated to the rear. (The Historical Society of the Somerset Hills)

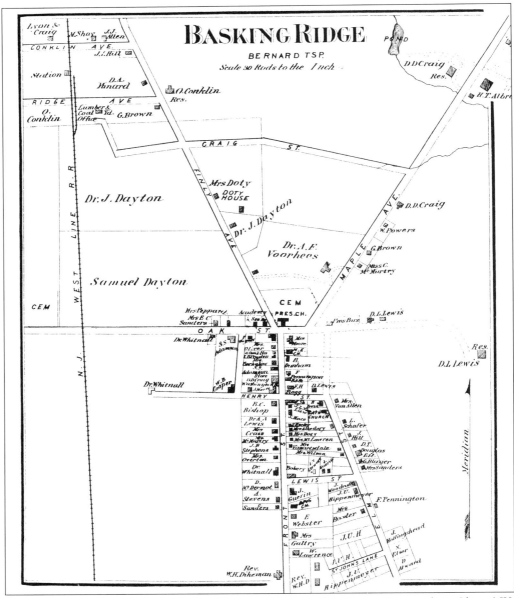

Basking Ridge village, from the *Atlas of Somerset County, N.J.* (Beers, Comstock & Cline, NY, 1873). See p. 102 for a directory of residents. (Bernards Township Library)

The Union Hotel, *c.* 1910. Located at the southwest corner of South Finley Avenue and West Henry Street, the hotel, originally an old tavern, was demolished in 1934. The Washington House can be seen on the right. (Bernards Township Library)

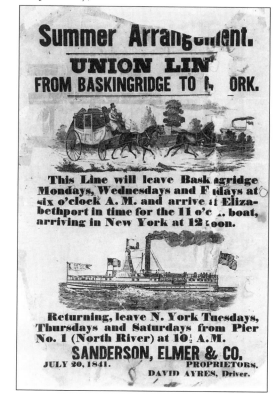

Travel from Basking Ridge, 1841. A "broadside" announced summer arrangements for travelers from Basking Ridge to New York City via coach and steamer. (The Historical Society of the Somerset Hills)

Mr. and Mrs. Calvin Thompson celebrated their fiftieth wedding anniversary with family and friends on the porch of their Madisonville Road home, 1895. (Mildred Dunham Van Dyke)

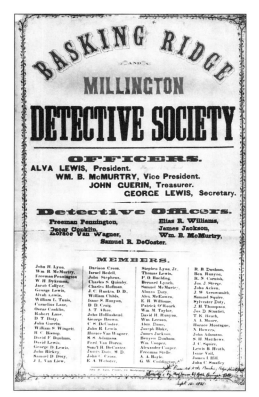

The Basking Ridge and Millington Detective Society, 1867. Forerunner of the present local police department, residents organized the society after the Civil War for protection. Many Township streets carry names of members of this group. (The Historical Society of the Somerset Hills)

Samuel R. DeCoster, *c.* 1900s, farmer and carpenter, at the family farm on North Maple Avenue. (DeCoster sisters)

The Enoch Howlett farm, at the foot of East Oak Street, *c.* 1910. The most ornate Second Empire house in Basking Ridge had fifteen rooms and was built about 1864 by Austin Cross. Its 156 acres included a barn for 40 cows. The Schaenen family owned the estate for many years. On the right were structures razed for Ridge Oak Senior Housing in the 1980s. (Fred Kampmier III)

The Carswell men in 1904. From left to right are John, Arthur, Bryce, Archibald Jr., and Archibald Carswell Sr. (Priscilla C. Bruno)

Washing Dixie, 1925. Bathing the dog at the Carswell home on Washington Avenue were, from left to right, Professor Harold Pfilicky, Doris Berman, Priscilla Carswell, Shirley Berman, and Janet Carswell. Professor Pfilicky was an uncle of the Carswells. (Priscilla C. Bruno)

Calvin Dunham's graduation from Princeton University, 1910. From left to right are J. Herbert Childs, Calvin Dunham, Sarah Bockoven, Edna Moore, Jane Dunham, John Turner, Edna Bockoven, Harold Bockoven, Raymond A. Henry, and Allan Connolly. (Mildred Dunham Van Dyke)

The Calvin Dunham family, 1918. From left to right are: (front row) Mildred and Margaret II; (back row) Emma, Charles, and Calvin. (Mildred Dunham Van Dyke)

The Orchard Farm, *c*. 1910. Built around 1870 at the corner of Madisonville Road and North Maple Avenue, this was the largest Second Empire-style house in Basking Ridge. For more than forty years, the Charles Roberts family lived there. Mr. Roberts, a prominent banker, was secretary/treasurer of the Childs Restaurant chain. (Mildred Dunham Van Dyke)

Charles Roberts (at the wheel) operating a right-hand drive automobile, *c*. 1915. The woman in the black hat at the rear was his cousin, Margaret Bergen Dunham, who later became the Township librarian from 1932 to 1963. (Mildred Dunham Van Dyke)

24

The third home of the Basking Ridge Free Circulating Library, 1905. From 1898 to 1908, through the generosity of Samuel S. Childs, 23 South Finley Avenue was adapted for library use. Mr. Childs built a community room with a stage and installed steel bowling alleys in the basement, with the fees to be used for library expenses. (Mildred Dunham Van Dyke)

William Pennington, M.D., 1894. After a successful medical career, Dr. Pennington volunteered as a book binder for the Basking Ridge Library. He is remembered for his detailed scrapbooks of local newspaper clippings in the Township Library. (The Historical Society of the Somerset Hills)

The Allen family, *c.* 1910. This was the home of James Walter Allen and Martha Holmes Allen and family at 174 South Finley Avenue. (William Allen)

Mr. and Mrs. Lewis Shafer and their granddaughter Ruth Shafer, *c.* 1915, at 64 South Maple Avenue. Mr. Shafer owned a men's tailoring shop which also housed the post office from 1898 to 1908. (Constance Carlson)

Cedar Hill was built by Samuel Owen as his country home on 100 acres in 1912. Of English Tudor design, it reflected his wife's British ancestry. Other owners were George L. Lee Sr., from 1940 to 1946; Eugene V.N. Bissell Sr., from 1946 to 1950; and John Jacob Astor VI, from 1950 to 1968. In 1968, the estate was bought by Bernards Township for a municipal complex, with all offices relocated there in 1975. (Township of Bernards)

Samuel Owen, *c.* 1930, a Newark pharmaceutical manufacturer and builder of Cedar Hill on Collyer Lane (see above). (Township of Bernards)

Picnicking in Owen's Woods, 1916. Owner Samuel Owen of Cedar Hill invited townspeople to enjoy his property and its flowering fruit trees. From left to right are Dorothy Wing, Jane Dunham, and Fred Runyon. (Mildred Dunham Van Dyke)

An aerial view of the estate and fruit orchards of the Cedar Hill Farm, 1935. The land is now the athletic fields of Ridge High School. The flowering fruit trees attracted many visitors, who also purchased the "drops." Superintendent Joseph Allenzo and his son Mario (on the tractor) are in the fields. (Mario Allenzo)

Enoch Howlett with his horse and buggy at Bishop Janes Methodist Church, *c.* 1910. The church's facade of natural stones was transported by congregation members from an area adjacent to the Great Swamp in 1899, with permission of the land owner, Colonel John Jacob Astor IV, who perished in the Titanic disaster in 1912. (*Historical Booklet of Bernards Township, N.J.*, 1960)

Mr. and Mrs. Ernest V. Hicks on their wedding day, February 27, 1919. Married by the Reverend Ira L. Ketchum of the Bishop Janes Methodist Church, the bride was the former Myrtle Wickenhaver. The building at right was the birthplace of William L. Dayton, lawyer, U.S. senator, and diplomat. (E.V. Hicks family)

Howard A. Brush and his family, *c.* 1917, on South Maple Avenue. From left to right are: (front row) brother James and sister Ruth Brush; (center row) sister Grace Brush, aunt Grace Dall, sister Jessie Brush, and mother Eliza Jane Brush; (top row) cousin Grace Dall, Howard Brush, grandfather Jesse A. Brush, and great aunt Sarah Bower. The building at the rear is the side of the original St. James Church. (Howard A. Brush)

The P.C. Henry General Store, *c.* 1890s. Built in 1860, it was a general store during the Civil War. In the early 1900s, a milliner's shop was on one side, and later a hardware store with a furniture showroom was above it. Now Brush's Market, it is a grocery, delicatessen, and convenience store. (The Historical Society of the Somerset Hills)

P. C. Henry

....DEALER IN....

...GENERAL...

Merchandise

✛✛✛

FURNITURE, MAT-
TRESSES AND ALL
KINDS OF BEDDING

✛✛✛

BASKING RIDGE ⚜ N. J.

J. Cooney & Co.

SUCCESSORS TO BOWERS & MOOSE

~ ~ BUTCHERS ~ ~

AND DEALERS IN

Choice Beef, Mutton, Lamb, Veal, Pork,
Poultry, Fish, Fruit, Vegetables.
Oysters & Clams In Season

BASKING RIDGE, N. J.

AERMOTOR

Galvanized Steel Wind-
mills, Towers.

Tanks and Substructures.

Pumps and Fittings

Gasoline Power, Pumping and Spraying Outfits

Complete Estimates on Water Supply and Power Outfits

P. C. McARTHUR, Basking Ridge, N. J.

Do you know that

⟶ We sell everything in the line of ⟵

Groceries, Flour, Feed, Crockery,
Boots, Shoes, Dry Goods, Neck
Wear, Stationery, Canned Goods.

etc., at the lowest market prices. Call and see us and be
convinced.

⟶ The City Store. ⟵

Henry Tobelman

Basking Ridge, N. J.

John W. Craig

Contracting Painter

Paperhanging a Specialty

BELL PHONE   ESTIMATES CHEERFULLY GIVEN
BASKING RIDGE, N. J.

GOLDEN RULE POULTRY YARDS

Single Comb Buff Leghorns, Partridge Plymouth
Rocks. The two great mortgage lifters.
Live and let live prices.

CHARLES M. and NED H. ALLEN

Basking Ridge, Somerset Co., N. J.

Washington... House

Raymond B. Trozell, Prop.
Successor to
Fred A. Nelson.

BILLIARD AND POOL PARLOR
CIGARS AND TOBACCO

FIRST CLASS ACCOMMODATIONS
FOR BOARDERS ⟶ Basking Ridge, N. J.

I. B. BOWERS,

DEALER IN

Choice Meats and Vegetables

POULTRY AND GAME IN SEASON.

BASKING RIDGE, N. J.

Reprinted ads, c. 1900s, from local newspapers and catalogs. (The Historical Society of the Somerset Hills)

Maple Lawn, *c.* 1910. The Hankinson family lived in this Mansardic-style house on East Craig Street, built in 1865, which has a colorful fishscale slate roof. (The Historical Society of the Somerset Hills)

The Monroe F. Ellis residence, *c.* 1908. This Gothic Revival home on North Finley Avenue was owned by Mr. Ellis, manager of the Conkling Lumber Company. Both Ellis Drive and Monroe Place were named for him. (Priscilla C. Bruno)

Marion Childs, c. 1912, feeding chickens at the McMurtry farm, on Hardscrabble Road in Franklin Corners. (Nancy Childs Knobloch)

Lillian and Arthur Roff with their son Donald, in front of the Oscar Roff barn on North Maple Avenue in 1913. (Elizabeth R. Sigler)

Donald A. Roff, *c.* 1925. He shoveled a path for neighbor Kate Happe at 52 East Oak Street, Basking Ridge. (Elizabeth R. Sigler)

Winter, 1934. An ideal sledding spot was the lawn of Orchard Farm, Madisonville Road, Basking Ridge. (Mildred Dunham Van Dyke)

The Frederick C. Sutro family, 1920. From left to right are Mr. Sutro Sr., Louis L., Elizabeth Winne Sutro, Frederick Jr., and Ogden W. Mr. Sutro was head of the New Jersey Parks and Recreation Association and was credited with fostering the Green Acres bond issue and the Garden State Parkway. He was active in local affairs and was the former president of the Bernards Township Board of Education. Sutro Place was named for the family. (Louis L. Sutro)

The Sutro brothers, 1939, at a cabin in the Palisades Interstate Park, where their father was executive director of the Park Commission. From left to right are Fred C. Jr., Ogden W., and Louis L. Sutro. (Louis L. Sutro)

The Coffee House, c. 1900. Located at the corner of Madisonville Road and North Maple Avenue, it was the center of the Madisonville hamlet, named for President James Madison. Originally built as a combination farmhouse, residence, and store, it was a tavern from 1814 to 1829 and the only social area within several miles. It is listed on the State and National Registers of Historic Places. (The Historical Society of the Somerset Hills)

Marion Stansbury Dayton and Kenneth A. Turner were married August 20, 1921, at the bride's family homestead at Coffee House Corner. (Marion D. Turner)

Part-time Bernards Township police, *c.* 1925. From left to right are Captain Bernard Richardson, Harold Pope, Clarence Stansbury, and Clyde Wolfe. In 1946 the Township appointed its first full time officer, W. Robert Moore. (William L. Scheuerman III)

Basking Ridge Fire Company No. 1, *c.* 1920. The first wooden firehouse cost $600 with labor and materials donated by citizens and members in 1905. (Mildred Dunham Van Dyke)

The residence of S.D. Conklin, *c.* 1920. The Colonial Revival-style house at 233 South Finley Avenue was built around 1905 and was the home of Dr. John Forbes in the 1950s. (Marion D. Turner)

Lew Day, *c.* 1925, Basking Ridge's mail messenger. (The Historical Society of the Somerset Hills)

Basking Ridge Fire Company No. 1 on its twenty-fifth anniversary, 1929. From left to right are: (seated, front row) John Pope, David Y. Moore, Frank McGuirk, and Bryce Carswell; (standing, middle row) Cazier Graback, Harold Fennimore, Fred Geiger, John Turner, Gordon Happe, Ernest Boss, Lewis Rickey, Ernest Bornmann, Harold Pope, Howard Hyler, and Vincent Masone; (standing, back row) George Crafferty, George Graback, Trueman Spencer, Thomas Maher, Wilbur Richardson, and John Carlson. (The Historical Society of the Somerset Hills)

The Basking Ridge First Aid Squad, 1935. Its first ambulance was a former hearse from the Garrabrant Funeral Home. From left to right are Robert Moffett, John Pope, Bryce Carswell, Henry Moore, and Lewis Rickey. (The Historical Society of the Somerset Hills)

Jeanette Cleveland McArthur with sons, *c.* 1900. From left to right are Peter, Robert, and Myron McArthur.(J. Donald McArthur)

The children of Peter and Sarah McArthur, *c.* 1930s. From left to right are John, Richard, Eleanor, Donald, and Fulton McArthur at their South Maple Avenue home. (J. Donald McArthur)

Peter McArthur, c. 1940s, Basking Ridge farmer and carpenter. (J. Donald McArthur)

Brick buildings identified as slave quarters on the site of Lord Stirling's estate, c. 1959. Recent studies concluded the structures were auxiliary buildings erected from materials of the manor house. (*Bernardsville News*)

I. F. GARRABRANT & SON, FUNERAL DIRECTORS AND EMBALMERS

The Ira F. Garrabrant Funeral Home, *c*. 1900. The property at 141 South Maple Avenue included a livery stable. Mr. Garrabrant was town clerk in 1901. (The Historical Society of the Somerset Hills)

Laying concrete, 1928. The South Maple Avenue project near Lord Stirling Road was one of the first concrete-paved roads in New Jersey. (J. Donald McArthur)

Nurse Elsie Bettler, *c.* 1922, on her graduation day from Morristown Memorial Hospital. (Phyllis Bettler Domanski)

M. Louise Henry, *c.* 1922, was a long-term history teacher at Bernards High School. She was the daughter of P.C. Henry (who owned the general store), and the sister of Raymond Henry (store manager) and Dr. Claire Henry (a Bernardsville dentist and mayor). (Agnes Dupay Sheehan)

The Wright family, 1911. The house at Oak Stump Corner where Oak Street joins Mount Airy and Pill Hill Roads was demolished in 1934. Mount Airy Road eventually replaced the Oak Stump address. From left to right are Leslie, Dorothy, Minnie, and Edward Wright. (Douglas Sloss)

The sons of William and Elsie Wright Sloss, 1927. The boys lived at Oak Stump Corner. From the top are Herbert, Wallace, and Douglas Sloss. (Douglas Sloss)

The DeCoster family, *c.* 1900, on North Maple Avenue. From left to right are: (bottom row) Lillie, Libbie, Douglas, Ella Dean, Gerald, Jennie Ella, and Charlotte; (top row) Frank E., Charles, Deborah B., Samuel R., Ethel, Atwood, and Ella. (DeCoster sisters)

Osborne's Pond, Basking Ridge, *c.* 1920. (Mildred Dunham Van Dyke)

The Childs family, 1915. Former New Jersey State Senator Samuel S. Childs was founder of the Basking Ridge Free Public Circulating Library and provided permanent quarters for the library. Celebrating the Childs' twenty-fifth wedding anniversary were, from left to right, daughters Mary and Lois, Samuel S., and Emma F. Childs. (Nancy Childs Knobloch)

Basking Ridge Library, c. 1940. The former session house and chapel of the Presbyterian Church at 2 North Finley Avenue was adapted by Samuel S. Childs and home of the library from 1909 to 1974. In 1930 Mrs. Childs had the structure brick-faced and donated the entire building to the library, as a memorial to her husband. The Somerset County bookmobile is on the left. (Bernards Township Library)

Winter, 1923. Brownlee Place, formerly Back Street, was covered with 3 feet of snow. The shovelers are, from left to right, Ray Wright, Emory Hancock, Howard A. Brush, and Ray Day. (Howard A. Brush)

The Joy Bearers Society of Bishop Janes Methodist Church, c. 1920s. From left to right are: (bottom row) Viola Mertz, Myrtle W. Hicks, Elizabeth Bunn, and Ruth Craig; (top row) Frances Wilcox, Mabel Wickenhaver, Marion Turner, and Etta Murray. (E.V. Hicks family)

The Washington House and Tunis Store, c. 1910, were two of the most popular places in Basking Ridge. The former, built in 1870, provided meals and lodgings and is now The Store Restaurant. Mr. Tunis' confectionary shop sold candy, newspapers, and had a soda fountain. (Mildred Dunham Van Dyke)

A pig roast, 1934. Pig roasts were a popular activity sixty years ago when farming was a major occupation. This roast was held behind the Washington House. From left to right are Lew Craig Sr., Bert Hankinson, P.J. Boyle, Marvin Parks, Joe Eggert, John Boyle, Hughes Hankin, and unknown. (*Bernardsville News*)

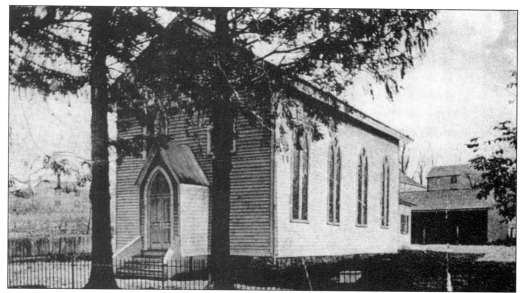

St. James R.C. Church, *c.* 1900. A carpenter shop in the mid-1800s on South Maple Avenue, it was adapted as a church and served parishioners until 1958 when it was demolished. Stables were located at the rear. The quaint white stoop at the right was for alighting from carriages or horses. In 1959 a new church was built on South Finley Avenue. (Agnes Dupay Sheehan)

Anthony P. and Marie B. Kearns, 1934, at their home on 395 South Finley Avenue, Basking Ridge. Mr. Kearns was a Somerset County District Court judge and for many years was the Township Attorney. (William J. Kearns)

The home of Halsey M. Larter, a wholesale jeweler, *c.* 1914. The property included 27 acres with 5 out-buildings, gardens, an orchard, and a tennis court. In the 1960s it became St. James Convent, the residence of a Felician religious order that conducts the adjacent parochial school of the church on South Finley Avenue. (Bernards Township Library)

The first commercial vehicle in Basking Ridge, 1912. Owned by Joseph Mueller, who ran a bakery/grocery business at the west end of Turner Street, the wagon could be converted into an open touring car. Mueller traveled to Philadelphia, bought the car, and drove it home without driving lessons or license! (The Historical Society of the Somerset Hills)

John V. Haas, *c.* 1900s, was a farmer, owner of the Sunnyside Farm, and the home agent of E.A. Strout Realtors. (Janet Haas McGahey)

The Haas family, *c.* 1905. From left to right are: (sitting) parents Susie McCollum Haas and John V. Haas; (standing) children J. Fred, Susie, and Annie Haas. The property is now the site of the Cedars town house development, off Valley Road. (Janet Haas McGahey)

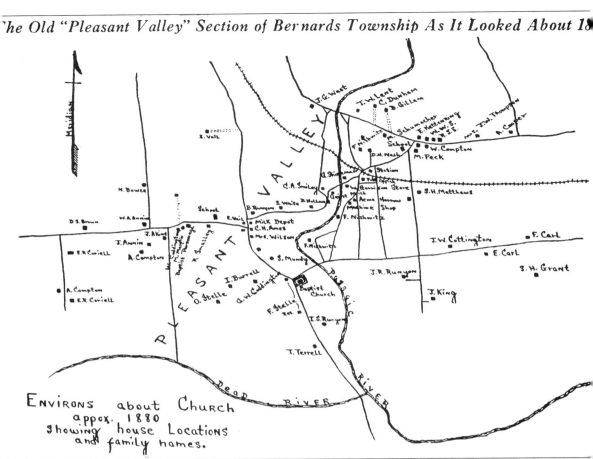

Pleasant Valley, 1880. This was the Millington area called Pleasant Valley; its schoolhouse was used as a meeting place of the Millington Baptist Church in its first year, 1851. The building is the present Carriage Inn Restaurant. (*Bernardsville News*)

A pattern book house, 1924. The "Vallonia", a bungalow, was ordered from a Sears Roebuck catalog and erected on Haas Road. The Honor Bilt home arrived via railroad at Millington. There are about two dozen various models in Basking Ridge. Another example is on Lord Stirling Road, now the residence of the manager of the Somerset County Park Commission's Environmental Education Center. (Denise Szabo)

Millington Baptist Church, c. 1901. Organized in 1851, the church is the third oldest in Bernards Township and is located at the corner of Valley and King George Roads, Basking Ridge. (The Historical Society of the Somerset Hills)

Air Mail Week, May 15–2l, 1938. Postmaster William L. Scheuerman Sr. accepts mail from George A. Viehman, pilot and manager of the Somerset Hills Airport, in front of a Taylor plane. The airport was built in 1932 on a large field owned by the Fenner family, who lived in the present Lord Stirling School building. After a 1981 fire, the airport was sold for town house development. (William L. Scheuerman III)

The Basking Ridge Post Office, c. 1930. The home of Postmaster William L. Scheuerman Sr. at 11 South Finley Avenue served as the post office for more than thirty years. A sign was suspended over the front steps. (The Historical Society of the Somerset Hills)

William Childs, *c.* 1930. Mr. Childs restored the Van Dorn Mill and Franklin Corners, a self-contained community of yesteryear, now a historic district and on the State and National Registers of Historic Places. (Bernardsville Library Local History Room)

The Van Dorn Mill, *c.* 1960. Called the finest stone work in New Jersey, it was built in 1843 and replaced a 1768 wooden structure. Thousands of stoneloads were hauled from the hedgerows of farms on Hardscrabble Road. Artisans were paid $1 per day to build the mill, which cost about $5,000 and paid for itself within the first year of operation. (*Bernardsville News*)

Raymond D. Moffett, 1936, at his car agency. An auto repair shop was at the South Finley Avenue site in 1924, with a new building erected in 1928. The showroom sign lists a GO Oldsmobile for $650. Car sales continue in this location today. (The Historical Society of the Somerset Hills)

Friends greet on Christmas Day, 1942. From left to right are June Skillman, Georgianna Crafferty, and Muriel Hicks. (June Skillman Martratt)

Loyal Robinson, c. 1940. Owner of Robinson's Gulf Service Station on Madisonville Road and Route 202, he was later a member of the Bernards Township Committee and was mayor in 1961, 1962, and 1964. (Peter S. Palmer)

The Henry family, c. 1950s, at 81 Conkling Street, Basking Ridge. From left to right are aunt Beatrice Garvin, Walter Henry, Ellen T. Henry, and Thomas Henry. (James Henry)

The Old Mill Inn, *c.* 1940, was the barn of the Van Dorn Mill. William Childs had it moved across the road in the 1930s and opened a restaurant, now called The Grain House. (The Historical Society of the Somerset Hills)

A Basking Ridge Gun Club picnic, 1940. From left to right are: (seated) Mrs. Kenneth Dunster, Vivian Dunster, Mrs. Art Petty, Mrs. Robert Garrabrant, Mrs. David Wright (with hat), Mrs. James Muldowney, Mrs. Calvin Sutton, Eleanor Masdale, Mrs. James Flynn, and Mrs. Charles Lum; (standing) Bert Hankinson, David Wright, Albert Magee, Kenneth Dunster, unknown, Donald Magee, George Snyder, John Muldowney, James Muldowney, William Coffin, James Flynn, Art Petty, Charles Fennimore, B. Armstrong, Calvin Sutton, and Charles Lane. In the front row, right, is Robert Fennimore. (The Historical Society of the Somerset Hills)

An aerial view of Basking Ridge, 1944. The World War II honor roll is on the village green. (William L. Scheuerman III)

Finley Avenue, the main thoroughfare in Basking Ridge, prior to World War II. (Priscilla C. Bruno)

Cousins, 1942. At a Wolsky family party on Mount Airy Road, Basking Ridge, were, from left to right: (front row) Tommy Wolsky, Rose Grabarczyk, and Bobby Wolsky; (back row) Rita Grabarczyk, Frank Wolsky, Mary Rose Wolsky, and Joseph Grabarczyk. (Elizabeth G. Wolsky)

Hannie Sanders Moore and David Y. Moore on their fifty-sixth wedding anniversary, 1954. The village blacksmith from 1898 to 1957, Mr. Moore could shoe as many as fifty-four horses in a ten-hour day. He was a charter member and fire chief of the Basking Ridge Fire Company. (Bernards Township Library)

The village blacksmith shop, 1950s. David Y. Moore was the last blacksmith in Basking Ridge and located at the corner of Dayton Street and North Finley Avenue. (Priscilla C. Bruno)

Jack DeCoste and family, 1952. From left to right are: (bottom row) Caroline and Paul; (middle row) Jim, Jack, and Bob; (top row) John and Dick. The family moved to Basking Ridge in 1937. (James DeCoste)

The village green, c. 1940. The veterans' monument faced the Presbyterian Church, with World War I mortar shells to the rear. The building on extreme right was the Cerino Brothers grocery, with the post office to its left. The green became public property in 1927 when the Cerinos deeded it to the Township, allowing only a flagpole and monument on the site. (Janet C. Arleo)

Arthur N. Starin and nephews, 1938. In front of the Alva Starin home at South Finley Avenue are, from left to right: (bottom row) Arthur Palmer Jr., Starin, and Hoyt Palmer; (top row) Roland, Ted, and William Palmer. (Peter S. Palmer)

The Christmas carol sing, 1959. The event was painted by Arthur N. Starin, an architect. The first carol sing on the green began in 1924 and attracts thousands annually. (Howard A. Brush)

The Basking Ridge Garden Club, 1961. Members displayed dried flower arrangements after a workshop. From left to right are Mrs. Carl Bergman, Mrs. Joseph Richie, President Mrs. Charles Evans, and Mrs. George Leaver. (Basking Ridge Garden Club)

The Old Oak Tree, c. 1920. Quercus Alba, a six-hundred-year-old tree in the Presbyterian churchyard, has been a travelers' landmark for generations: Washington and Lafayette picnicked under it; colonial troops enjoyed its shade; and thirty-five veterans of the American Revolution are buried beneath it. The oldest burial was in 1737. (Bernards Township Library)

A foreign policy study group of the Bernards Township League of Women Voters, 1959. From left to right are Mrs. Philip Fagans Jr., Mrs. C.W. Raycroft, Mrs. Charles Brasher, Mrs. Thomas Reynolds, Mrs. Robert Fortenbaugh, Mrs. Donald Kelly, Bethania Tucker, Mrs. William W. Bradley, Mrs. Jack Niedner, Mrs. L.W. Day, and Mrs. Brock Lewis (chairman), reading a report. (League of Women Voters Somerset Hills)

The Bernards Township's 200th Anniversary Parade, May 21, 1960. The marchers are approaching the Presbyterian Church. There were record crowds with floats and bands adding to the festivities. At right, directing traffic in a white shirt with his back to camera, is Patrolman Harry Allen, who would later become the chief of police. (The Historical Society of the Somerset Hills)

The company plane, 1959. George Ludlow Lee Sr., chairman of Red Devil Tool Company, donated 60 acres of land for the Cedar Hill and Ridge High Schools and 12 acres of land for the War Memorial Field. From left to right are unknown, son John Lee, George L. Lee Sr., unknown, son George Lee Jr., and son Todd Lee. The plane was sold after Mr. Lee's death in 1966. (George Lee III)

The superintendent's cottage on South Maple Avenue, 1960, part of the John Jacob Astor VI estate. (Paul Sempf)

Two

Liberty Corner

Liberty Corner, 1905. Arthur Burnett's hotel can be seen on the left, with Acken's General Store and Post Office at the head of Church Street. In the background was the Acken house; in Revolutionary times, this was Bullion's Tavern. (Woodruff J. English)

The main farm of the numerous branches of the Annin family, from which Annin's Corner and Annin Road derived their names. In considering the accuracy of old prints and illustrations, one must always allow for artistic license, the reliability of the artist, and the intention of the person who paid for the work. (The Historical Society of the Somerset Hills)

The old stone house built by William Annin in 1766 of material from a neighboring quarry. During the American Revolution, Annin's house was used as a church, school, hospital, and recreation center. He later became a member of the New Jersey State Legislature. The house was located off Lyons Road. (Bernards Township Library)

The Liberty Corner Presbyterian Church, c. 1890. Built in 1869 by James P. Goltra, it was the second structure of the congregation. (George L. Frost Collection)

Reverend James T. English (1810–1873). Dominie English was the first pastor of the Liberty Corner Presbyterian Church, from 1838 to 1873. (The Historical Society of the Somerset Hills)

William and Catherine Saunders, at 32 Church Street, Liberty Corner, 1890s. The house was built around 1800. Mr. Saunders was the first sexton of the Presbyterian Church, and served for thirty-eight years. (Shirley Ehrenberg)

Phoenix Gutleber, a local tradesman and merchant, c. 1900s. Mr. Gutleber was delivering an order on Church Street, Liberty Corner, with its wooden sidewalks and hitching posts. (Mary Guest Kenney)

The Liberty Corner Presbyterian Church choir, Christmas, 1910. From left to right are unknown, unknown, Anna Winken Meigh, Martha Dobbs Frost, unknown, Mary Elizabeth Frost, unknown, and Lizzie Nuse Dobbs. In 1897 Lizzie Dobbs was the church organist. (George L. Frost Collection)

James Phares Goltra (1792–1871), a carpenter and builder. Mr. Goltra constructed the Liberty Corner Presbyterian Church in 1869 at age seventy-seven; he erected many churches in the Somerset/Hunterdon area. He was a successful farmer and merchant, judge of the Court of Common Pleas, and helped enlist recruits during the Civil War. (Bernards Township Library)

The Acken General Store and Post Office, across from the Liberty Corner village green, c. 1898. Charles Acken bought the building at age twenty-two, and worked there until his death in 1948. In 1893 he was appointed postmaster by President Cleveland and reappointed by Presidents Wilson, Harding, Coolidge, Hoover, and Roosevelt. (Laurence Smith)

The installation of wooden sidewalks on Church Street, Liberty Corner, 1898. (Bette King Sisto)

The Jacob Guest house on Liberty Corner-Far Hills Road, *c.* 1889. The structure burned in the late 1920s; on its site is the Richard Kenworthy farm. From left to right are Amos Guest, Jay Guest, Robert Guest, and grandfather Jacob Guest. In the rear is grandmother Anna Foster Guest. (Mary Guest Kenney)

The Daniel King homestead on Allen Road, looking east in Liberty Corner, *c.* 1910. The house in the center is the Pinson home and formerly was the Deeney farm. Aside from the demolition of the barns and the return of open fields to scrub growth, this area has changed very little. (George L. Frost Collection)

A horse and carriage by the rear porch of the English homestead at 3625 Valley Road, Liberty Corner, *c.* 1905. From left to right are Conover English, William Hall, and Ella Jane English. The horse was called Bob. (Woodruff J. English)

The English family by the front porch of the homestead at 3625 Valley Road, *c.* 1905. From left to right are Conover English (son of Ella Jane), cousins Mary and Elsie Jobes, Ella Jane Hall English (mother of Conover), and Nicholas Conover Jobes English (grandfather of Conover). (Woodruff J. English)

The house at 26 Church Street, Liberty Corner, late 1800s. Donald and Eretta Baldwin Douglas owned this house from 1920 to the 1990s. The cow probably was purchased at an auction and its owner was escorting it home. The people are unidentified. (Deborah Juterbock)

Eretta Baldwin Douglas (1891–1993). A life-long resident of Liberty Corner, she attended a one-room schoolhouse on Lyons Road, was a kindergarten teacher in Bernardsville, and substituted locally. Mrs. Douglas was active for decades in the Liberty Corner Presbyterian Church. (Deborah Juterbock)

Harriet King Tewes and Henry N. Tewes at their Church Street, Liberty Corner house in 1917. Mr. Tewes was a local farmer. (June Skillman Martratt)

Donald Douglas (1891–1968) of Liberty Corner, 1910. A skilled carpenter, he erected homes in Bernards Township and was building inspector for three years. His family lived on Douglas Road, which was named for them. Mr. Douglas married Eretta Baldwin in 1916. (Deborah Juterbock)

Samuel G. Crane (standing) and Frank
Ransford Crane, *c.* 1890s. They were
sons of Mr. and Mrs. George A. Crane
of Annin Road, Liberty Corner.
(Ransford G. Crane)

Boys strolling down Church Street stopped at the Liberty Corner Presbyterian Church (at left)
in the early 1900s. (Deborah Juterbock)

Catherine Ortman Crane and George A. Crane of Annin Road, Liberty Corner, *c.* 1910. (Ransford G. Crane)

The Crane homestead on Annin Road, *c.* 1918. From left to right are Samuel G., Catherine O., Frank R., George A., and Mabel Crane. (Ransford G. Crane)

The Seilor Brothers Creamery was located less than 200 feet from the historic Annin stone house. A fire at the dairy in 1893 almost destroyed the 1766 home, still in "a most excellent state of preservation." Many creameries supplied rich dairy products to Newark and New York hotels via the railroad. (Bette King Sisto)

The Liberty Corner village green, c. 1906. The general store on the right was owned by C.C. Acken. (Bernardsville Library Local History Room)

The Liberty Corner Fire Company, incorporated in 1910, was inactive because of a lack of funds until 1915. Land was bought and a building constructed on Church Street (the lot cost $200 and the headquarters $1,087). Bernardsville donated the first apparatus, a hook and ladder wagon pulled by hand or towed behind the Koechlein delivery truck. The second floor was used for Bernards Council #242, Jr. Order United American Mechanics. The bell was from the Mount Prospect School. (The Historical Society of the Somerset Hills)

"Old Number One," an American La France fire truck, 1932, was greeted with comments such as "It's too big for the town." It replaced a 1924 Ford and took the firemen five years to pay for the new equipment. (The Historical Society of the Somerset Hills)

The Liberty Corner Fire Company, March 26, 1937. From left to right are: (front row) Joseph Stantial, William Swody, Charles P. Bird, Norman Looker, Henry Tewes, Harold Apgar, Russell Teeple, John Smith, Chief Philip Koechlein, Joseph Happe, Robert Acken, Augustus Coddington, Samuel Crane, Charles Anstedt, Philip Anstedt, and Harold Gehling; (back row) Harold Croot, Voorhees Acken (at wheel), Thomas Allen, John C. Bird, and George Acken. (Philip Koechlein)

The dedication of the new Liberty Corner Fire House, July 14, 1956. New Jersey State Senator Malcolm Forbes was guest speaker at the ceremonies. (Carolyn Graham Malfatone)

Compton House, later the David King homestead, c. 1893, is the oldest residence in Bernards Township. From left to right are: (in wagon) Harlan A. King and Georgia R. King; uncle William King, Melissa Blazure, grandchild Arthur R. King, and grandmother Adeline E. King. (Bette King Sisto)

Arthur Randolph King and Elizabeth Bunn King with their daughter Elizabeth Dent King, at their Church Street home, The Magnolias, April 1930. (Bette King Sisto)

Best friends Elsie Wright (left) and Leona Froehling of Liberty Corner, *c*. 1916. (Douglas Sloss)

The residence of Julius Froehling, Liberty Corner, *c*. 1910. The house was across from the village green at the junction of Lyons Road and Church Street. (Carolyn Graham Malfatone)

Frances DeWitt of Phillipsburg and Voorhees Acken of Liberty Corner on their wedding day, August 14, 1928. Mrs. Acken graduated from Trenton Normal School in 1919 and stayed with Ada Allen in the village; she was the first teacher to live in the newly-constructed teacherage, built in 1923, adjacent to the Liberty Corner School. (Laurence Smith)

Three generations of Ackens in Liberty Corner, 1935. From left to right are Mary Acken, Charles C. Acken, their son Voorhees Acken, and their sixteen-month-old granddaughter Lois Acken, in the wheelbarrow. (Laurence Smith)

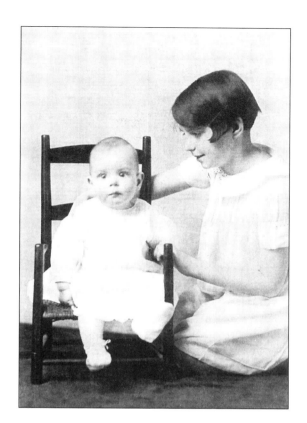

Betty Douglas with her brother Ronald, 1929. They were children of Donald and Eretta Baldwin Douglas of Church Street, Liberty Corner. (Deborah Juterbock)

A Douglas family party, c. 1930s. From left to right are: (front row) Betty, grandparents John and Margaret Douglas, and Ronald and Kenneth Douglas; (rear row) uncle Rob, aunt Mae, Robert, Donald and Eretta Douglas, and uncle Howett. (Deborah Juterbock)

Fair View River Farm, *c*. 1910. Herbert Hilmer Sr. bought the farm and house on the east side of Martinsville Road, south of the Dead River in 1915. This is now site of the Chubb Insurance office. (The Historical Society of the Somerset Hills)

The Hilmer family at Fair View River Farm, Liberty Corner, 1934. From left to right are Marie, Herbert Jr., mother Emma, Doris, father Herbert Sr., and Pauline. (Herbert Hilmer Jr.)

Schley Glider Field, at the end of Mount Prospect Road, Liberty Corner, on Labor Day weekend, 1933. Note the trophies on the table at left. The annual event was initiated by the South Orange Glider Club and attracted thousands. Liberty Corner Boy Scouts operated the refreshment stands as a fund raiser. (Marion G. Stadtmueller)

The first-class campers of Liberty Corner Troop 54 at the Watchung Council Camp-O-Ral overnight, May 29, 1936. The troop's first scoutmaster was Harold Dobbs. From left to right are: (kneeling) Arthur Burton, Hank Martin, and Peter Martin; (standing) Edson Beatty and Don Meeker. (Laurence Smith)

Mr. and Mrs. Charles C. Acken, *c.* 1938. Mr. Acken was proprietor of Acken's General Store. (Laurence Smith)

The only double-stone arch bridge in Liberty Corner, *c.* 1908. It was on the Martinsville Road where it crossed the Dead River. (The Historical Society of the Somerset Hills)

Phareloch Castle, Somerville Road, Liberty Corner, *c.* 1920s. Designed and built by William and Frank Beatty on 180 acres, the French Normandy-style chateau later became Woodcastle School, Chartwell Manor School, Wildwood Castle, Castle Utopia, and Burlingame Castle. W. Beatty was an architect/advertising executive. F. Beatty was Bernards Township Mayor in 1930 and acting Lyons Hospital Postmaster. In the early 1970s, the castle was partially destroyed by fire. Sanford Road was its address in the 1930s. (Bob, Bill IV, Barbara, and Gail Beatty)

Bob, Bill IV, and Barbara Beatty sitting on a stone wall of Castle Phareloch, Liberty Corner, 1940. (Bob, Bill IV, Barbara, and Gail Beatty)

The Harold Gehling family at their Valley Road, Liberty Corner home on Christmas Day, 1941. From left to right are: (front row) daughters Mary, Edith, and Lois; (back row) sons Robert and Harold Jr., mother Edith, father Harold Sr., and sons George and Russell. (Lois Gehling Martin)

Harold Gehling Sr. of Valley Road, Liberty Corner, served as part-time police chief of Bernards Township in the mid-1940s. (Lois Gehling Martin)

P.J. Koechlein's General Store, Church Street, Liberty Corner, *c.* 1904. This was where the first telephone in the village was located, where the first movies in the area were viewed, and where the first commercial ice cream was sold. Note the wooden sidewalks and telephone sign. (*Historical Booklet of Bernards Township*, 1960)

Philip J. Koechlein and his sister Madeline were storekeepers for fifty years and retired in 1971. The store's telephone received the calls for the Liberty Corner Fire Company. Mr. Koechlein, with sisters Grace and Madeline, sounded the fire alarm until 1969. (*Bernardsville News*)

Miriam Haas and Robert W. Olsen were married at the Liberty Corner Presbyterian Church on December 24, 1939. The bride wore the wedding dress of her great-great-grandmother. (Janet Haas McGahey)

Alan Jaquish and Gloria Hippchen of Mendham cut their wedding cake following the ceremony at the Whitenack Road home of the Jaquish family, March 24, 1948. (Alan Jaquish)

The George Acken farm in Liberty Corner, c. 1908, site of the original Fellowship Deaconess' home. Prior to 1940, the road between Liberty Corner and Martinsville followed the present driveway into the Deaconry, passed in front of this house, and joined Allen Road several hundred feet to the west of the present Martinsville Road. (The Historical Society of the Somerset Hills)

The Fellowship Deaconry administration building, c. 1940. Established in Liberty Corner in 1933, the Deaconry includes modern guest houses, a chapel, a conference center, a children's camp, several farm buildings, a bookstore, a branch of the Philadelphia School of Bible, and Fellowship Village, a continuing care center presently under construction. (Bernards Township Library)

Maple Lodge, Church Street, Liberty Corner, 1932. Charles Venick, proprietor, is at right. The car is a 1928 Ford. (Rosemary Allen)

J. Fred Haas and his sister Susie Haas Bryan, 1935. In the background is a quilt made by the Dead River Sunday School class of the Liberty Corner Presbyterian Church. Janet Haas McGahey has the quilt. (Janet Haas McGahey)

John and Esther Little Happe in their Valley Road home, Liberty Corner, 1935. Mr. Happe was superintendent of the English farm. (Lois Gehling Martin)

The hay barracks on the N.C.J. English farm, *c.* 1905. Superintendent John Happe (at far right) is shown with a helper and milk cans on the cart. (Woodruff J.English)

The Baldwin Farm, Liberty Corner, was a late eighteenth-century saltbox residence on Church Street. (Deborah Juterbock)

Samuel and Antoinette Boyle Baldwin of Liberty Corner, *c.* 1940s. Mr. Baldwin (1869–1935) was the first chief of the Liberty Corner Fire Company and also Bernards Township's Tax Assessor. (Deborah Juterbock)

The women of the Liberty Corner Presbyterian Church, late 1940s. From left to right are Eretta Douglas, Grace Warren, Charlotte Frost, Edna Crane, Elizabeth Suhr, and Marion Frost (with her back to the camera), the hostess at her Mount Airy Road home, Bernardsville. (Deborah Juterbock)

Country Cousins, a theatrical group of the Liberty Corner Presbyterian Church, raised funds for several years and met socially, c. 1960s. From left to right are: (front row) Ada Allen and Alice Lare; (middle) Madeline Aspray; (back row) Frances Acken, Muriel Wetzel, Katherine Graham, Edna Crane, and Edna Nielson. (Carolyn Graham Malfatone)

Carolyn, Curtis, and Eunice Graham, the children of Herbert and Katherine Graham, at their home at 454 Lyons Road, Liberty Corner, 1941. (Carolyn Graham Malfatone)

Liberty Aviaries, c. 1946, was owned by Herbert Graham, who sold pet birds and canaries from 1940 to 1950 at 454 Lyons Road, Liberty Corner. Mr. Graham was a Township Committeeman in 1950. From left to right are Carolyn Graham, Elizabeth Acken, and Eunice Graham, with Curtis Graham in the front. (Carolyn Graham Malfatone)

Girl Scout Troop #ll, Liberty Corner, at its second anniversary party, 1947. From left to right are: (first row) Stephanie Lantz, Marie Kaiser, unknown, Barbara Coleman, Janet Nielson, and Carmen Ansede; (second row) unknown, Eunice Graham, Mary Szarek, unknown, Martha Anstedt, Jackie LeCoultre, and Helen Curley; (third row) Edna Burke (assistant leader), Lois Acken, Judy Woznak, Gay Howell, Edna Burke (leader), Jane Coddington, Lillian Anstedt, Edith Gehling, Joan Bettler, and Carol Pearson; (back row) Rita Grabarczyk, unknown, and Jean Burke. (Laurence Smith)

This building was the Liberty Corner Post Office from 1962 to 1975. It had been a private residence and was reported to have belonged to a sea captain. The present post office is located on the same site. Prior locations were Allen Hotel/Burnett house, and the Koechlein and Acken General Stores. (*Bernardsville News*)

Bernards Township's 200th Anniversary, 1960. The parade through Liberty Corner passed Koechlein's General Store on Church Street. (The Historical Society of the Somerset Hills)

John Compton's blacksmith shop, c. 1910. The shop was on the first floor, with the rest of the building and rear space occupied by J.N. Irving, wheelwright. Both structures were razed in 1920. (George L. Frost Collection)

Dignitaries at the Liberty Corner village green, 1960, during the Township's 200th Bicentennial. From left to right are Committeemen Merle Chamberlain, Warren Craft, David Meeker, Loyal Robinson, Mayor William Badgley, Clerk Charles Anstedt, and William L. Scheuerman Jr., chairman of the Bicentennial Committee. (William L. Scheuerman III)

The Golf House of the U.S. Golf Association since 1972, the Georgian red brick mansion was built for the Thomas Frothingham family in 1919. The John Sloan family called it Pastureland in 1930. The site includes a museum and library, administration building, and a research and test center on 62 acres. Its cottage is the country home of Cyrus and Grace Sloan Vance. (*Bernardsville News*)

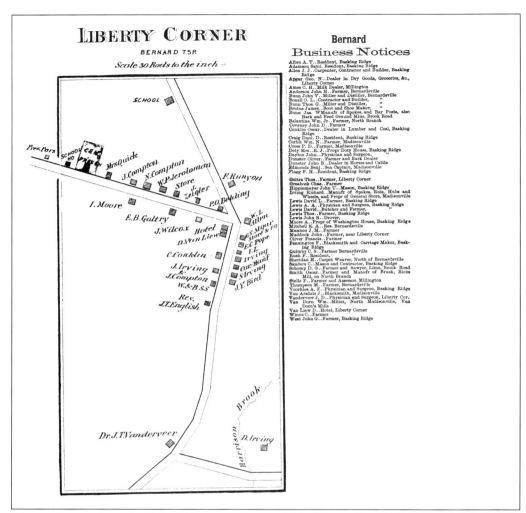

LIBERTY CORNER

BERNARD TSP.

Scale 30 Rods to the inch

Bernard
Business Notices

Albro A. T..Resident, Basking Ridge
Adamson Saml. Resident, Basking Ridge
Allen J. J..Carpenter, Contractor and Builder, Basking Ridge
Apgar Geo. N..Dealer in Dry Goods, Groceries, &c., Liberty Corner
Ames C. H..Milk Dealer, Millington
Anderson John H..Farmer, Bernardsville
Bunn John V..Miller and Distiller, Bernardsville
Bonell O. L..Contractor and Builder, "
Bunn Thos. G..Miller and Distiller, "
Brutus James..Boot and Shoe Maker; "
Bunn Jas. W Manufr of Spokes, and Bar Posts, also Bark and Feed Ground Mine, Brook Road
Balantine Wm. Jr.. Farmer, North Branch
Coveney John D.. Farmer
Conklin Oscar..Dealer in Lumber and Coal, Basking Ridge
Craig Danl. D..Resident, Basking Ridge
Corbit Wm. N.. Farmer, Madisonville
Cross P. D.. Farmer, Madisonville
Doty Mrs..R. J.. Propr Doty House, Basking Ridge
Dayton John..Physician and Surgeon,
Dunster Oliver..Farmer and Bark Dealer
Dunster John B..Dealer in Horses and Cattle
Edmonds Benj..Sea Captain, Madisonville
Flagg F. H..Resident, Basking Ridge

Goltra Thos..Farmer, Liberty Corner
Greabock Chas..Farmer
Hippinmayer John U..Mason, Basking Ridge
Irving Richard..Manufr of Spokes, Ruis, Hubs and Wheels, and Propr of General Store, Madisonville
Lewis David L..Farmer, Basking Ridge
Lewis A. A..Physician and Surgeon, Basking Ridge
Lewis David..Butcher and Farmer, "
Lewis Thos..Farmer, Basking Ridge
Lewis John R..Drover,
Moore A..Propr of Washington House, Basking Ridge
Mitchell H. A..Res. Bernardsville
Mannon J. M..Farmer
Maddock John..Farmer, near Liberty Corner
Oliver Francis..Farmer
Pennington F..Blacksmith and Carriage Maker, Basking Ridge
Quimby C. S..Farmer Bernardsville
Rush F..Resident, "
Sheridan H..Carpet Weaver, North of Bernardsville
Sanders C..Mason and Contractor, Basking Ridge
Schomp D. G..Farmer and Sawyer, Lime, Brook Road
Smith Oscar..Farmer and Manufr of Brush, Blobs Mill, on North Branch
Stelle F..Farmer and Assessor, Millington
Thompson M..Farmer, Bernardsville
Voorhies A. F..Physician and Surgeon, Basking Ridge
Van Arsdale J..Blacksmith, Madisonville
Vanderveer J, D..Physician and Surgeon, Liberty Cor.
Van Dorn Wm..Miller, North Madisonville, Van Dorn's Mills
Van Liew D..Hotel, Liberty Corner
Winne C..Farmer
West John G..Farmer, Basking Ridge

Liberty Corner, from the *Atlas of Somerset County, N.J.* (Beers, Comstock & Cline, NY, 1873). Because of space constraints, this directory lists Basking Ridge residents of the map on p. 18. (Bernards Township Library)

Three
Lyons

SCENE AROUND LYONS, N. J.

The scene around Lyons, *c.* 1910. This could be on the Passaic River or Harrison's Brook. Since the barn has an advertisement for Ceresota Flour, there must have been a main road, either on the right hand side of the photograph or running across the far side of the stream passing the barn. The exact Lyons location is unknown. (The Historical Society of the Somerset Hills)

The Lyons Railroad Depot, c. 1915. This structure was replaced with a Norman-influenced building in 1931. (The Historical Society of the Somerset Hills)

The Lyons Railroad Station. In 1931 the Delaware, Lackawanna and Western Railroad built a new depot at Lyons, which featured Norman-style architecture that combined brick and stucco with multipane casement windows, slate roof, steep gables, and copper-hooded bay windows. The station, a typical example of early twentieth-century eclecticism, was the last one added on the D. L. & W. line. (The Historical Society of the Somerset Hills)

Martha and Angelo Ruggerio with their son James, 1906. These Columbia Road, Lyons, residents were photographed prior to visiting relatives in Airola, Italy. Eight other children were born to the family. (Carmen Ansede Fortenbacker)

The main house at Coppergate Farm, Lyons Road, c. 1900. (Bernardsville Library Local History Room)

The stone crusher, *c*. 1908. This was used in daily quarry operations; the facility is the present Millington Quarry on Stone House Road, Lyons. (*Bernardsville News*)

The Commonwealth Quarry Company, *c*. 1920s. Workers stand outside the Wash and Change Building. Samuel Ruggerio of Lyons is at the rear center with the dark hat. The company later became the North Jersey Quarry Company, the Houdille Quarry, and is now the Millington Quarry. (Mary Ruggerio)

Helen and Harold Thomson, 1916, children of Mr. and Mrs. James Thomson, Lyons Road. Mr. Thomson, a realtor/insurance owner, constructed homes on the east side of Lyons Road, from Stone House Road to Byron Drive. Harold Thomson later became the mayor of Bernards Township. (Helen Thomson Smith)

Helen Thomson of Lyons and John Dayton Smith of Peapack on their wedding day, 1935. Attendants were Jack Pierson (left) and Edith Killey. The Smith family was among Peapack's earliest settlers. (Helen Thomson Smith)

107

The home of Luther and Anna McMurtry Childs, c. 1900s. This residence off Lyons Place later became Two Brooks Farm. Its barns were dairy buildings for the Childs Restaurants. (Nancy Childs Knobloch)

Marion, Samuel, baby Nancy, and Louise Childs, 1926. The children of J. Herbert and May Belle Post Childs, they were photographed at their home, Midfield, in Lyons. In 1912, Mr. Childs was Lyons Postmaster. (Nancy Childs Knobloch)

The U.S. Veterans Hospital, c. 1930s. With legislation passed by the 68th Congress in 1925, the hospital at Lyons opened in 1930 to treat World War I veterans from New Jersey, western New York, eastern Pennsylvania, and the Brooklyn Naval Hospital. The hospital's property includes more than 300 acres and has a patient population of about 1,000. (Bernardsville Library Local History Room)

Governor A. Harry Moore (left), with straw hat, arrived at the Somerset Hills Airport in 1932 to visit the U.S. Veterans Hospital at Lyons. Greeting him in the white shirt is manager and head instructor, Wally Shantz. To the right are members of the New Jersey State Police. (J. Donald McArthur)

Antoinette Ruggerio (left) and her sister Rose were bridal attendants at this Lyons wedding, c. 1931. (Carmen Ansede Fortenbacker)

The Delaware, Lackawanna and Western grade crossing at Lyons, 1930. The railroad line was often called the "Delay, Linger and Wait Railroad." (Homer and Jean Hill)

Leroy Stinson and his daughter Mae, 1931. Mr. Stinson was the groundskeeper/chauffeur of the Freer estate at Lyons called Bontecoe Farm, adjacent to the Coppergate Farm. Mr. Freer had a cottage built on Lyons Place as the Stinson residence. (Mae Stinson Ruggerio)

The Freer estate, c. 1930s. This was the home of Hugh and Bessie Freer at the corner of Lyons Road and Wharton Way. The original section of the house was built in the mid-nineteenth century. In the past decade, a stone facade has been added. (Nancy Childs Knobloch)

Rose Ruggerio and Frank Ansede, c. 1932, shortly after their marriage. (Carmen Ansede Fortenbacker)

The Ansede family, 1943, on the stone bridge at Columbia Road, Lyons. From left to right are John, Richard, Frank Sr., Frank Jr. (in front), Rosemarie, and Rose Ruggerio Ansede. (Carmen Ansede Fortenbacker)

Coppergate Farm, c. 1949. Owned and operated as a dairy farm on Lyons Road by Frederick W. Beinecke, it was sold to the Day family. Thomas Florio purchased it and conducted a riding stable and equestrian school for more than two decades. The barn was moved to Liberty Corner. Custom-built homes now occupy the site. (Paul Sempf)

The Millington A.C. Football Squad, 1948. The Crimson Tide continued as a team, after graduation from Bernards High School. From left to right are: (kneeling) Ernie Cummings, Warren Oppel, Pete Ruggerio, Charles Domanski, Steve Carfaro, Lou Pavao, Pat D'Apolito, Mac Lowery, and Barney Flynn; (standing) Edward J. Black (coach), Atlas Mastrobattista, Hap Compton, Ted Harvey, Harry Allen, Foster Ensminger, Charles Manailovich, Larry Ferratti, Bob Flynn, Bill Richardson, Frank Beatty, Ed Carroll, Eugene Fennimore, Ray Falls, Dick Liddy, Frank Carfaro, Vic Mastrobattista, and Sal Trepiccione. (Rosemary Allen)

Carmen Ansede and Charles Fortenbacker of Lyons were married in the original St. James R.C. Church on South Maple Avenue, July 14, 1956. A member of the Bernards Township Police Department since 1955, Fortenbacker is Bernards Township Chief of Police. (Carmen Ansede Fortenbacker)

Four

School Days

Third and fourth grades, Maple Avenue School, Basking Ridge, 1914. The teacher, Sarah Bockoven, can be seen in the back. (The Historical Society of the Somerset Hills)

Brick Academy, c. 1900. Built in 1809 as the Basking Ridge Classical School, it prepared young men for the College of New Jersey (Princeton University). It has also been a public school, union hall, town hall, and serves as an area museum. (The Historical Society of the Somerset Hills)

Dr. Robert Finley was the fifth pastor of the Basking Ridge Presbyterian Church, from 1795 to 1817, and solicited funds to build the Brick Academy for his classical school. Dr. Finley became president of Franklin College (University of Georgia at Athens) in 1817 but died before the start of the first semester. (The Historical Society of the Somerset Hills)

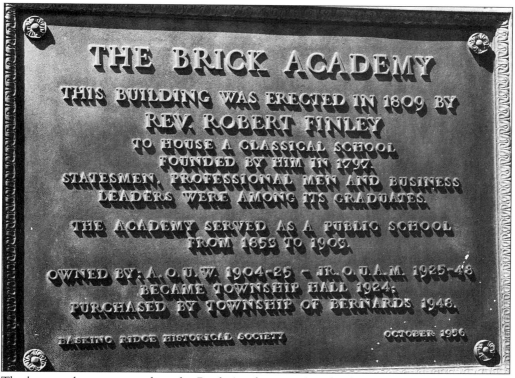

THE BRICK ACADEMY
THIS BUILDING WAS ERECTED IN 1809 BY
REV. ROBERT FINLEY
TO HOUSE A CLASSICAL SCHOOL
FOUNDED BY HIM IN 1797.
STATESMEN, PROFESSIONAL MEN AND BUSINESS
LEADERS WERE AMONG ITS GRADUATES.

THE ACADEMY SERVED AS A PUBLIC SCHOOL
FROM 1853 TO 1903.

OWNED BY: A.O.U.W. 1904-25 — JR.O.U.A.M. 1925-48
BECAME TOWNSHIP HALL 1924.
PURCHASED BY TOWNSHIP OF BERNARDS 1948.

BASKING RIDGE HISTORICAL SOCIETY   OCTOBER 1956

The bronze plaque mounted on the Brick Academy, 1956. This building is listed on the State and National Registers of Historic Places. (*Bernardsville News*)

Students of School District #12, 1895, on the steps of the Brick Academy, West Oak Street, Basking Ridge. The school was used from 1853 to 1903 when Maple Avenue School was completed. (The Historical Society of the Somerset Hills)

Eighth graders of the Basking Ridge Grammar School, 1909. This was the first class that entered Maple Avenue School and graduated in 1910. From left to right are: (front row) Dorothy Connolly, Marion Roberts, Mary Waldron, Myra Howlett, Marion Dayton, Frances Wilcox, Mildred Bennett, Lillian Bornmann, and Viola Sanders; (back row) Britton Everett, Charles Karston, Russell Pope, Carroll Allen, Willett Neer (principal), Garret Rutman, Charles Ehrler, and Leonard Bender. May Petty and Jessie Hendershot were absent from the photograph. (Marion D. Turner)

Maple Avenue School, 1910. Built in 1903, a second floor was added in 1909. It was a school until 1939 when Oak Street School was opened. Later leased by the school board from Bernards Township from 1948 to 1969, it was demolished in 1973 to provide space for the present Bernards Township Library. (Priscilla C. Bruno)

Anna D. Merrell, 1900. Miss Merrell taught at the one-room Mount Prospect School; she became Mrs. Amos Guest and was the mother of Mary Guest Kenney, later the principal of the Liberty Corner School. (Mary Guest Kenney)

The Mount Prospect School, c. 1900. The school was abandoned upon completion of the Liberty Corner School in 1905. The school bell was donated to the local fire company and was in service until 1920. In 1947 the building was moved on Liberty Corner-Far Hills Road and converted into a house. (Jean Hill)

The Liberty Corner School, 1905. The village long suffered from cramped school conditions. The new building had two large rooms, which measured 24-by-28 feet with 12-foot-high ceilings, and cost $7,600. In 1915 another room and an additional teacher were added for pupils of the then defunct Pleasant Valley School. Four additions have since been built. (The Historical Society of the Somerset Hills)

The Liberty Corner School, 1906. The students are Ed Froehling, Pearl Stantial, Ora Haines, Art King, Charlotte Frost, Ella Lare, Belle Acken, Alma Haines, Marion Allen, Addie Woods, Minnie Allen, Olga Gutleber, Tom Allen, George Green, Andrew Martin, Elmer David, Henry Wright, Laura Martin, Hattie Thompson, Elsie Wright, Sibylla Wright, Fred Fee, and Gladys Burnett. The teachers are Miss Elliott and Miss Harmon. (Philip Koechlein)

A horse-drawn school bus, c. 1910. This transportation was used by Liberty Corner students attending Bernards High School. There were many times when the bus toppled over! (Deborah Juterbock)

The Liberty Corner School, 1909. From left to right are: (bottom row) Frank Werner, Lloyd King, Alice Gutleber, Margaret Allen, Kathy Sanders, Steve Graback, Philip Koechlein, George Ferris, and George Baldwin; (middle row) Ethel Trimmer, Voorhees Acken, George Hoffmeister, Mary Rose Kearns, Ruth Riker, Dorothy Werner, Hazel Bird, Helen Fee, Leona Froehling, Elsie Wright, and Sibylla Wright; (top row) George Gieseke, Christine Riddle, Ethel Stantial, George Riker, Henry Hamfeldt, teachers Martha Dobbs Frost and Gertrude Willard, Carl Doeges, Robert Hamfeldt, Anthony Kearns, William Lampe, and Jeff Hoffmeister. (Deborah Juterbock)

Church Street, c. 1925. The white building at right was the teacherage, erected in 1923 as housing for teachers. The faculty was paid about $1,200 a year, and could not afford to buy a car or horse and buggy. The teacherage was needed because rooms were scarce. William J. Howes (principal) and his wife Grace A. Howes (who would later become principal) paid $30 per month rent. In the mid-1950s, the teacherage was razed to provide playground space. It was one of the last such buildings in New Jersey. (Laurence Smith)

Liberty Corner school teachers, 1939–40. From left to right are Mary Guest Kenney (third grade), Catherine Schmelzer (first grade), and Grace A. Howes (sixth grade). (Marion G. Stadtmueller)

The Liberty Corner School, 1926. From left to right are: (bottom row) Nellie Grabarczyk, Elizabeth Sawyer, Betty Douglas, Bertha Rinehart, Alice Walters, Sarah Rinehart, Antoinette Ruggerio, Philomena Carfaro, and unknown; (middle row) Alice Luck, Beth Warren, Martha Kruger, Edythe Croot, unknown, unknown, Margaret Burnett, and Anna May Bryan; (top row) Billy Burnett, Tommie DeMott, Clifford Weber, John Wojnar, and teacher Miss Coe. (Deborah Juterbock)

The Liberty Corner School, c. 1900s. The school was built at the bend of the road leading from Liberty Corner center to Lyons, as indicated on an 1870 map. The school was demolished in 1970. (Bernards Township Library)

May Day, 1919. Students from Basking Ridge, Liberty Corner, Bernardsville, and Far Hills participated in this annual celebration at the Far Hills Fair Grounds. Every school's colored streamers were wound around a May pole (blue and gold were Basking Ridge colors, with yellow and white for Liberty Corner). Exercises included Indian clubs, track and field events, group calisthenics, baton drills, hoops, and other acrobatic feats. The buses in rear provided transportation. (The Historical Society of the Somerset Hills)

The Maple Avenue School faculty, 1915. From left to right are: (seated) Sue Tuttle and Irma Siebert; (standing) Agatha Greulock, Elizabeth Steele, Willett Neer (principal), Minnie L.Tewes, and Sarah Bockoven. (Priscilla C. Bruno)

The seventh and eighth grades, Maple Avenue School, 1921. From left to right are: (bottom row) Sadie Channing, Ruth Mast, Elida Abel, Edna Mast, Pauline Saebic, Viola Richardson, Eva Bailey, and Helen Peterson; (middle row) Mary Craig, Edna Cline, Jenny McPherson, Bertha Wenmen, Harriet Snable, Annie Jancie, Violet Richardson, and Henrietta Buck; (top row) Carrie Snyder, Stanley G. Wilson (principal), Frank Dubus, Walter Bettler, Chester Moore, Harold Thomson, Albert Snable, Samuel Saebic, Robert Garrabrant, Clayton Emmons, Alan Craig, and George Graback. (The Historical Society of the Somerset Hills)

The second and third grades, Maple Avenue School, 1923. From left to right are: (bottom row) Christine DeForest, Katherine Sansone, Dorothy Flint, Elizabeth Dobbs, Margaret Bennett, Doris Berman, Catherine Scheuerman, Rosalie Enyingi, Lennart Carlson, and L. Brown; (middle row) James Graback, unknown, unknown, Louis Enyingi, Ellsworth Sanders, Gordon Fennimore, Edward Jones, unknown, and B. Peterson; (top row) Robert Moffett, Lionel Corbin, William Upshaw, Bernard DeCoster, James Thomson, Jack Hankinson, and Charles Snyder. (Constance Carlson)

First graders of the Maple Avenue School, 1924. From left to right are: (bottom row) Lorraine Wolfe, Shirley Berman, Janet Carswell, June Merritt, Nellie Fennimore, unknown, Helen Riker, unknown, and Edson Riker; (top row) Ransford Crane, Alexander Truppi, Thomas Fargey, unknown, William Scheuerman, Frank Graback, Austin Spencer, Eddie Jones, Fenn Crafferty, and Sidney Brown. The teachers are Sarah Bockoven and Miss Light. (Priscilla C. Bruno)

The Maple Avenue School baseball team, 1930. From left to right are: (front row) Robert Moffett, Ellsworth Sanders, Bud Seimor, Moonie Hill, and James Thomson; (back row) Eddie Hill, Billy Blood, Jack Twitchell (principal), William Thompson, Monroe Peterson, and Herbert Shauger. The team won 4 and lost only 2. (Priscilla C. Bruno)

The eighth grade of the Maple Avenue School, 1925. From left to right are: (bottom row) Steve Optruchak, Alex Enyingi, Donald McArthur, Fulton McArthur, George Browne, Harry Petty, and John Allen; (middle row) Helen Thomson, Jessie Brush, Frances Thorpe, Ruth Wrigley, Ann DeCoster, Helen Snyder, Alice Sauer, and Aranka Slezak; (top row) Harry Katerman (principal), Ruth Buck, and Agatha Graback. (The Historical Society of the Somerset Hills)

The Maple Avenue School orchestra, 1932. From left to right are Violette Oppel, Priscilla Carswell, Eleanor Burnett, Jack B. Twitchell (principal), Eric Johnson, Richard McArthur, and Douglas Struck. (The Historical Society of the Somerset Hills)

The Maple Avenue School eighth grade graduation, 1934. From left to right are: (front row) Kelton Jones, Bryce Carswell, Sheridan Combs, John McArthur, Willis Scheuerman, Jack Zakarian, Roy Snable, Ed Geisel, Richard Ostrander, and Otto Truppi; (middle row) Bernice Lowe, Judith Koenichneck, Natalie Howlett, Jessie Farcey, Betty Ross, Marie Bennett, Alvina Kampmier, and Rose Marion Head; (back row) Irene Parsons, Margaret Enyingi, Helena Jones, Jack B. Twitchell (principal), Ruth Thompson, June Skillman, and Pat Small. (June Skillman Martratt)

The Oak Street School, 1939. Built on a 12-acre tract, the school was described as the finest and most modern in Somerset County. A public works grant and bond issue amortized over twenty years paid for construction. Children marched from the Maple Avenue School to Oak Street in a parade. Additions were built in 1952, 1989, and 1994. (*Bernardsville News*)

Eighth graders of the Oak Street School, 1947. From left to right are: (front row) Francis Condon, Nancy Grove, Nancy Bauries, Nancy Snable, Connie Kamper, and Al Davenport; (second row) teacher Eunice Clark, Bill Leslie, Connie Schaenen, Don Ross, Grace Allen, Roland Francisco, and teacher Louise Flint; (third row) Arthur Ward, Jack Westervelt, Mary Shoppe, Barbara Metcalf, Janet Shauger, Florence Park, Edward Muldowney, and Tom Condon; (back row) Louise Cox, Charles Hertz, Ed Guest, Jack B. Twitchell (principal), Jerry Fernicola, Kurt Hedel, Bob Craig, and Pat Twitchell. (The Historical Society of the Somerset Hills)

Oak Street students as Township officials, 1950. From left to right are: (front row) Junior Committeemen Joseph Brush 2nd, Donald Vander Wyde, and Earl Polan; (second row): Junior Clerk Donald Davis, Assessor Chris Ward, Tax Collector Robert Beringer, Health Board Secretary Margaret Connolly, Engineer David Koppes, Road Superintendent John Deinert, Attorney William Aitken, Police Chief Leonard Rembo, and Magistrate Carole Kennedy; (back row) Attorney Anthony P. Kearns, Engineer Kenneth A. Turner, Collector Scott F. Tarner, Assessor Robert Gutleber, Committeeman Herbert W. Graham, Mayor Harold B. Thomson, Warren M. Craft, Police Chief W. Robert Moore, Principal Jack B. Twitchell, and Clerk Charles E. Anstedt. (Helen Thomson Smith)

Pirates of Penzance, Oak Street School, 1952, staged by the upper grades. James DeCoste is on the ship's bridge (top right); Donald Watson is at far right. (James DeCoste)

Bonnie Brae, c. 1927. The private non-profit year-round residential and educational center has been on Valley Road since 1920. It serves neglected and abused New Jersey boys, ages eleven to eighteen. (Bonnie Brae)

The Lord Stirling School, 1970. This school has educated pupils with emotional problems in ungraded classes since 1964. The original structure was built in the mid-eighteenth century and was reputed to have been a guest house of Lord Stirling's estate. (Lord Stirling School)

Five

Patriotic Times

The Town Hall at 15 West Oak Street, Basking Ridge, was decorated for Bernards Township's 200th Anniversary celebration, May 2l, 1960. Since 1975, all local government offices are located at the municipal complex, 1 Collyer Lane, Basking Ridge. (Orrin Lincoln)

William Alexander, Lord Stirling (1726–1783), in a portrait by Bass Otis. Stirling was third in command of colonial troops during the American Revolution. He was first to enlist in the Somerset County militia, formed his own unit, and fought in all of the colonies except Georgia and South Carolina. Stirling entertained many notables at his estate. An agriculturalist, entrepreneur, and amateur scientist, he contributed much to this area and to the Revolutionary cause. His death prior to the war's end cost him the fame he would have earned in the new America. (Independence National Historic Park)

Stirling Manor. In 1761, Lord Stirling began construction which was never completed because of the American Revolution. The estate was considered one of the most grandiose in the Colonies; it eventually fell into disrepair. (From a needlework of Katherine Wright, 1784)

Sir Francis Bernard was royal governor of New Jersey from 1758 to 1760. Because of his diplomacy in resolving disputes in the French and Indian War, King George II created by charter Bernardston Township. Bernard's successor was Sir Thomas Boone, ancestor of Daniel Boone, the frontiersman, and Pat Boone, the entertainer. (Massachusetts Historical Society)

The arrest of General Charles Lee, December 13, 1776. Lee, second in command of American troops, left his men at Jockey Hollow and spent the night at the Widow White's Tavern.The British hid in the fields across the road, now site of St. James Convent, and arrested him. Later exchanged, he insulted Washington at the Battle of Monmouth in 1778; Lord Stirling presided at Lee's court martial. (The Historical Society of the Somerset Hills)

Mary E. Lewis of Basking Ridge sewed this sampler in 1773 at the age of nine. She later married Joseph Kinnan and was captured by the Shawnee Indians in western Virginia, 1791. Her husband and two children were massacred; her brother Jacob escaped with her two sons and returned to Basking Ridge, where funds were raised for her rescue. Lewis eventually found his sister in Detroit and brought her home, where she became a legend. Known as "Aunt Polly," she lived to be eighty-four years old. (Jonathon Booth, a direct descendant of Lewis family)

The tombstone of Mary Lewis Kinnan (1764–1848) in the Basking Ridge Presbyterian Church cemetery, North Finley Avenue side. (Bernards Township Library)

Samuel Lewis Southard (1787–1842). Southard was born in Basking Ridge, and was a graduate of the Basking Ridge Classical School. He later became a U.S. Senator, governor of New Jersey, secretary of the Navy, and a justice of the New Jersey Supreme Court. He and his father, Representative Henry Southard, authorized the Missouri Compromise legislation in Congress. (Township of Bernards)

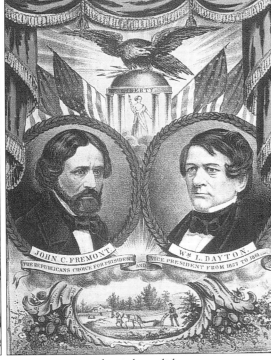

Two Basking Ridge Classical School graduates were vice-presidential candidates.
Left: In 1844 U.S. Senator Theodore Frelinghuysen was running mate of Henry Clay. Frelinghuysen was later president of Rutgers College. (The Historical Society of the Somerset Hills)
Right: U.S. Senator William Lewis Dayton was running mate of John C. Fremont in 1856. Dayton was the U.S. ambassador to France during the Civil War. (*Abbeville Press*)

American Legion Neill Card Post #114, Basking Ridge, was named in honor of two World War I casualties. Sergeant William B. Neill (left) Company F., 311th Infantry, 78th Division, was killed in action at St. Michiel, France, on September 30, 1918. Private Arthur Card, 18th Company, 5th Regiment, U.S. Marines, was gassed at Chateau Thierry, France, and died on July 6, 1918. (The Historical Society of the Somerset Hills)

The Bernards Township militia, 1919. Supported and supplied by John A. Roebling, the group was drilled and trained by Lieutenant Joseph Dobbs (far right). Mr. Stryker (center) stands as sergeant along side the trained troops. (Bernardsville Library Local History Room)

Basking Ridge firemen at the July 4, 1918 parade. From left to right are William Richardson, Chester A. Carling, Ned O. Howlett, and Leport F. Dunster. (The Historical Society of the Somerset Hills)

Spirited sentiments against Germany during World War I were reflected at the 1918 carnival of the Basking Ridge Fire Company, with a booth called "Soak the Kaiser." (Nancy Childs Knobloch)

Mr. and Mrs. Arthur R. King at a Liberty Corner patriotic celebration, 1925. (Bette King Sisto)

The Basking Ridge Historical Society, 1940. Members model costumes of the Civil War period at an historic pageant. From left to right are: (front row) Mrs. Henry Livingston, Frances Cornish, Constance Lance, Mrs. Charles Allen, and Mrs. Isaac Combs; (back row) Mrs. Arch Carswell (president), John D. Carswell, Mrs. Eldridge Jolliffe, Bernice Lowe, Peggy Lance, Mrs. Henry B. Hill, Helene Sutro, Mrs. John D. Carswell, Mrs. Charles Cornish, and Mrs. David Y. Moore. (The Historical Society of the Somerset Hills)

Lieutenant Austin P. Spencer of Basking Ridge, U.S. Naval Air Corps, was lost at sea in the North Atlantic while flying a Vega Venura bomber on submarine and convoy duty in 1943. He was the son of Tax Collector and Mrs. Trueman H. Spencer. Spencer Road was named in his honor. (Homer Hill)

Sergeant George E. Brush of Basking Ridge, U.S. Marine Corps, was killed in action on Guadalcanal, South Pacific, 1944. (Howard A. Brush)

Private Andrew F. Grabarczyk of Liberty Corner, U.S. Marine Corps, First Division, was the first Somerset Hills World War II serviceman killed in action. He died in the Battle of Guadalcanal in 1942. (Marion G. Stadtmueller)

Amelia Grabarczyk and her three servicemen sons, 1944. From left to right are Frank, U.S. Navy; Anthony, U.S. Navy; and Peter, U.S. Marine Corps. (Marion G. Stadtmueller)

Captain Robert Terry, flight instructor for the Tuskegee Airmen from 1941 to 1945, taught young Afro-Americans to fly P-39 and P-40 fighter planes, and trained others to pilot the B-52 bombers at the U.S.A.A.F. base in Alabama. In the 1950s, Captain Terry was chief pilot/instructor at the Somerset Hills Airport. (Qaaim Saalik)

Brothers James (left) and Harold Thomson of Lyons, returned from war duty, 1945. James was a U.S. Navy pilot in both World War II and the Korean War. Harold was in the U.S. Army Corps of Engineers and was the mayor of Bernards Township in 1950, 1951, 1953, and 1956. (Helen Thomson Smith)

Veterans' monument and flag pole, Liberty Corner, 1949. The dedication was held during the Memorial Day services. To the right is the Acken General Store and Post Office. (Carolyn Graham Malfatone)

Liberty Bell in Liberty Corner, 1950. A replica of the bell toured New Jersey promoting Savings Bond sales and was displayed at the Liberty Corner Presbyterian Church. From left to right are Reverend William D. Amos, pastor emeritus, and Reverend George R. Cox, pastor. (Carolyn Graham Malfatone)